GAI

CENGAGE Learning

Novels for Students, Volume 11

Staff

Editor: Elizabeth Thomason.

Contributing Editors: Anne Marie Hacht, Michael L. LaBlanc, Ira Mark Milne, Jennifer Smith.

Managing Editor: Dwayne D. Hayes.

Research: Victoria B. Cariappa, *Research Manager.* Cheryl Warnock, *Research Specialist.* Tamara Nott, Tracie A. Richardson, *Research Associates.* Nicodemus Ford, Sarah Genik, Timothy Lehnerer, Ron Morelli, *Research Assistants.*

Permissions: Maria Franklin, *Permissions Manager.* Jacqueline Jones, Julie Juengling, *Permissions Assistants.*

Manufacturing: Mary Beth Trimper, *Manager, Composition and Electronic Prepress.* Evi Seoud, *Assistant Manager, Composition Purchasing and Electronic Prepress.* Stacy Melson, *Buyer.*

Imaging and Multimedia Content Team: Barbara Yarrow, *Manager*. Randy Bassett, *Imaging Supervisor*. Robert Duncan, Dan Newell, *Imaging Specialists*. Pamela A. Reed, *Imaging Coordinator*. Leitha Etheridge-Sims, Mary Grimes, David G. Oblender, *Image Catalogers*. Robyn V. Young, *Project Manager*. Dean Dauphinais, *Senior Image Editor*. Kelly A. Quin, *Image Editor*.

Product Design Team: Kenn Zorn, *Product Design Manager*. Pamela A. E. Galbreath, *Senior Art Director*. Michael Logusz, *Graphic Artist*.

Copyright © 2001
Gale Group
27500 Drake Rd.
Farmington Hills, MI 48331-3535

ISBN 0-7876-4894-9
ISSN 1094-3552

Printed in the United States of America.
10 9 8 7 6 5 4 3 2 1

Watership Down

Richard Adams 1972

Introduction

Watership Down was first published in 1972, when Richard Adams had almost given up on having it published at all without resorting to paying for the publication out of his own pocket. The book, which originally began as a series of stories Adams told to his two young daughters on long car trips, was originally published by a small press, Rex Collings, and then reprinted by Penguin as a juvenile title, and by Macmillan as an adult title. Surprisingly, Adams's tale of a band of adventurous rabbits became a huge success, and eventually won the Guardian Award and the Carnegie Medal. The book's success led to a great surge in the publication of other fantasies set in animal communities. Adams was not the first writer to use animals as his main characters, and noted that the animal stories of Ernest Thompson Seton served as inspiration for the book. However, *Watership Down* had the rare distinction of being read by both children and adults and of receiving wide critical acclaim. In the *International Companion Encyclopedia of Children's Literature*, Peter Hunt called the book "the most successful single postwar [World War II] animal story."

Watership Down is not a sweet fable about bunnies; it's a gritty, often frightening tale, in which characters die or become injured and these facts of life are not disguised. Hunt quoted an interview with Adams, in which Adams said of his writing style, "I derived early the idea that one must at all costs tell the truth to children, not so much about mere physical pain and fear, but about the really unanswerable things—what [writer] Thomas Hardy called 'the essential grimness of the human situation.'" Paradoxically, Adams chose a tale about rabbits to do just that.

Author Biography

Richard George Adams originally began telling the story of *Watership Down* to his two young daughters, Juliet and Rosamund, during long car trips. A civil servant in Britain's Department of Environment, Adams was interested in nature and concerned about the environment, and these interests are strongly apparent in the book, which tells the story of a group of rabbits who are forced from their home by real estate development.

Adams's daughters insisted that he publish the book, which took two years to write, but it was rejected by thirteen major publishers. Discouraged, Adams considered paying a publisher to print the book, but then heard of Rex Collings, a small publisher who had just produced a book about animal characters. Rex Collings accepted *Watership Down* and agreed to print 2,000 copies. From this modest beginning, the novel's merits spread by word of mouth among avid readers, and it was later reprinted by Penguin and Macmillan, with huge success. The book won the Guardian Award and the Carnegie Medal, and it is regarded by many as a classic of fantasy.

Richard George Adams was born May 9, 1920, in Newbury, Berkshire, England, where the book is set, and attended Bradfield College in Worcester. He received a B.A. in modern history there and earned an M.A. at Worcester College, Oxford. He served in the British Army from 1940 to 1945, and then obtained a post as a civil servant in the Ministry of Housing and Local Government in London, and was assistant secretary of the Department of the Environment until 1974, when he became a fulltime writer. He has been a writer-in-residence at the University of Florida in Gainesville and at Hollins College in Virginia. In addition, he has served as president of the Royal Society for Prevention of Cruelty to Animals. He and his family have lived in London and in a cottage near the Berkshire Downs, where the events in *Watership Down* take place.

Since writing *Watership Down*, Adams has written many other books, including *Shardik, The Plague Dogs, The Girl in a Swing, Maia, Traveller*, and many other titles, including nature guides and collections of fables. He has also written an autobiography, *The Day Gone By*.

A Vision of Blood

Watership Down tells the story of a small group of rabbits who leave their home, Sandleford Warren, at the urging of Fiver, a young, small rabbit who has the gift of clairvoyance and who has a vision in which the entire field where the warren is located is covered in blood. His vision is correct: the area is soon to be bulldozed and developed, and the warren will be destroyed by humans. Although most of the rabbits think they are safe and ignore Fiver's warning, a few believe him, and they set out, led by Fiver's brother Hazel, a calm and modest yearling. They head south, toward the far-off hills Fiver says will be a safe home.

Dangers along the Way

They face various hazards posed by predatory animals, such as a badger, a dog, crows, and foxes; by terrain, as they cross the Enborne River; and by humans, who have guns and cars. At a temporary rest stop, they are digging rough shelters in a meadow near the river when a well-fed, aristocratic rabbit named Cowslip appears and invites them to join his warren, which is not far off. This invitation is strange and contrary to rabbit ways, and they are initially suspicious, but eventually decide to go with him to the warren.

Too Good to Be True

The new warren is a strange place: the rabbits there are all as sleek and rich as Cowslip, and they provide the wanderers with comfortable burrows and good food, but they also all seem vaguely sad, and none of them will ever answer a direct question. This secrecy is disturbing to Hazel, Fiver, and the others, but since they can find nothing obviously wrong with the warren, they are tempted to stay there. The temptation lasts until they find out that the warren's apparent safety from predators and its abundant supply of food are the work of a nearby farmer, who leaves food out for the rabbits and shoots predators that would hunt them, but who also occasionally kills some for his own use. The rabbits in the burrow have chosen safety and wealth in exchange for their freedom and perhaps their lives, but when Bigwig, a strong and capable member of the wanderers, is caught in a snare, the wanderers realize the danger they are in and head out. Strawberry, a member of the new warren whose mate has been recently snared, also decides this price is too great to pay, and joins them.

A New Home on Watership Down

At Fiver's urging, the group climbs a high hill, known as Watership Down, and within a grove of beeches, begins digging the warren that will be its permanent home. The site is ideal: high and remote, so the rabbits can see predators from far away, and at some distance from the dangerous humans.

Although these male rabbits are not accustomed to digging warrens—a task usually undertaken by female rabbits—the work makes them realize that they have become a strong team and that Hazel is a compassionate, intelligent, and capable leader. Shortly after they move in, two straggling survivors show up—rabbits who did not follow Hazel's initial warning and who stayed in the original warren, and who were there when humans poisoned and bulldozed it. These survivors are Holly, former captain of the Sandleford security force, or Owsla, and Bluebell, a young rabbit with a never-ending supply of bad jokes.

Plans for the Future

Although the rabbits now have a new home, they soon realize that their community will not last long without female rabbits and future generations to sustain it. They discover Kehaar, a wounded seagull who is lingering in the neighborhood until his wing heals, and make friends with him. In gratitude, when he is healed he agrees to fly around and reconnoiter the landscape, then come back and tell them where they can find female rabbits, or does. He reports two locations: Nuthanger Farm, where tame rabbits are kept in cages, and Efrafa, a large wild rabbit warren to the south.

The rabbits decide to send Holly and some others to that warren so that he can ask for does. While they are gone, Hazel and a small rabbit, Pipkin, go to the farm. Although they succeed in liberating two tame does there, Hazel is wounded and lost in a drainage pipe, and is only found and healed through Fiver's second sight.

Efrafa

Holly and his group return, badly shaken by their experiences at Efrafa, the large warren. The warren is a totalitarian dictatorship, run by General Woundwort, a strong and ruthless rabbit who refuses their request for does and also tries to trap and keep them in Efrafa, which is a closed society.

Hazel, undaunted, devises a plan. Bigwig goes to Efrafa, pretending to be a loner who is looking for a new home in a strong society. He infiltrates the Efrafa secret police and is accepted by Woundwort, and meanwhile works to find does who are dissident and who would be willing to leave Efrafa. These are not hard to find, because it's such an oppressive society, but getting them out safely is the challenge, as the warren is highly regulated and every move is watched. With Kehaar's help, the rabbits pass news and strategy back and forth between Bigwig and Hazel, and plan the escape from Efrafa.

A Valiant Escape

With the help of a thunderstorm, Kehaar, and a boat that a human has left on the river, Bigwig and the others run a frightening and nick-of-time course away from Woundwort and his ruthless security officers. Even after they arrive home, they find that

Woundwort and his forces are still pursuing them and plan to lay siege and battle them until they are dead, in order to get the dissident does back. The enemy rabbits start digging into the new warren, and Bigwig leads the fight against them valiantly; he is almost killed by Woundwort. Hazel and other rabbits run to Nuthanger Farm, where they gnaw through the watchdog's rope and then lead him back to the warren, where he attacks Woundwort and his minions. Woundwort is killed, although his body is never found. Hazel, who was wounded back at the farm, is found by a little farm girl, nursed back to health, and brought back to the warren in a car by the girl and a local doctor who advises her that he is a wild rabbit and will be happier in the wild; thus, he returns in triumph.

The Efrafan survivors of the raid are allowed to join the Watership Down warren, and the group of rabbits, now safe, grows and prospers. By the end of the book, future generations of rabbits listen in awe to the tales of their forebears, mingled with frightening stories of General Woundwort and the rabbits' age-old mythologies.

Characters

Bigwig

Bigwig is a large, powerfully built rabbit, originally a member of his home warren's "Owsla," or police force. His name, Thlayli, literally means "furhead," a reference to the distinctive thick growth of fur on the top of his head. At first, the other rabbits are wary of him; when Hazel brings up his plan to leave the home warren, he is taken aback when Bigwig volunteers to come along. Adams writes, "The last thing Hazel had expected was the immediate support of a member of the Owsla. It crossed his mind that although Bigwig would certainly be a useful rabbit in a tight corner, he would also be a difficult one to get along with. He certainly would not want to do what he was told— or even asked—by an outskirter."

Although Bigwig is used to being respected and has a tendency to throw his weight around, as the rabbits' adventure progresses, he proves that he certainly is "a useful rabbit in a tight corner." In the new warren, the rabbits realize that they need female rabbits to carry on, or their community will not live beyond one generation. Bigwig's major role in the book involves his leadership of an expedition to an enemy warren to get doe rabbits, during which he shows not only great courage and physical strength, but also quick yet calm thinking. In the expedition, he goes alone to the warren, called Efrafa, pretending to be a loner looking for a new home in a disciplined community. Having ingratiated himself with the secret police there and pretending to be an enthusiastic member of their group, he makes friends with a dissident female rabbit, Hyzenthlay, and uses the cover of a thunderstorm and the help of a seagull, Kehaar, to lead a group of ten discontented does to safety. The escape is fraught with danger, but the group makes it to the new warren.

Arriving at their new home on Watership Down, Bigwig and the does settle in to recover from their exhausting trek, but soon find that General Woundwort, leader of Efrafa, has followed them and intends to battle over the does. Laying siege to their burrow, he sets his forces to work digging into the Watership Down warren, and Bigwig comes to its defense. He is almost killed in a personal fight with Woundwort, but in the end, with the help of all the rabbits and a dog, the Watership Down rabbits win the battle.

By the end of the book, through all these adventures, Bigwig has matured into a fair but still powerful figure in the new warren, under the leadership of Hazel. Described as "a hulking veteran, lop-eared and scarred from nose to haunch," in the final pages of the book he is teaching the new young rabbits of the warren how to deal with cats and other hazards, as a sort of benevolent old soldier.

Blackberry

Blackberry is a very clever rabbit, whose mind is quick and inventive. When the group has to cross a river, he notices an old sign on the bank and realizes that it must have drifted downstream: therefore, it must float. He also realizes that if a rabbit stands on it, the rabbit will float too: the wood can serve as a raft. Most of the other rabbits are not able to understand this, but they trust his intelligence and are able to use the wood to cross the river. Later, they use a boat in a similar manner to escape pursuit by General Woundwort and his forces. Blackberry also figures out how to open a cage that holds some does on a farm, and later participates in a dangerous quest to release a dog tied on a nearby farm and lead it to attack Woundwort and his forces.

Cowslip

Cowslip offers the wandering group shelter at his warren. When they meet him, they see that he is "a big fellow, sleek and handsome. His fur shone and his claws and teeth were in perfect condition.... There was a curious, rather unnatural gentleness about the way in which he waited for them to come nearer.... He had the air of an aristocrat." Despite this, he also has an aura of sadness about him, which puzzles the wanderers. They are further puzzled by the inhabitants of his warren, who are all equally well-fed, equally sad, and who produce art, architecture, and poetry, all of which are foreign to the rougher, traveling band of rabbits. He invites them to stay in his warren, saying that there is plenty of empty space in it, and they will be welcome there.

This puzzles them, since rabbits are usually more territorial, and eventually they discover that the good food and safety from animal predators come at a price. A nearby farmer, noticing the warren of rabbits, puts out food for them and kills predators, thus ensuring their safety, but periodically he also snares and kills some of them to sell in the market. The rabbits in the warren are aware of the price they pay, but are too comfortable to want to change it; the farmer only takes a few, and each rabbit hopes and assumes it will be someone else. Cowslip, in inviting them, knows that they will probably be killed, since they don't know about the snares—so his invitation is a death sentence in disguise. Fiver feels the menace, but his vision of the danger is not clear enough to prevent Bigwig from being caught in one of the snares.

Fiver

Fiver is an undersized rabbit, the "runt" of a large litter, whose rabbit name, "Hrairoo," literally means "Little Thousand," or "the smallest of many." Although stunted in size, Fiver is large in spirit and has a prophetic gift: he is clairvoyant, and often sees events at a distance or in the future. Because of this gift, he is often high-strung and sensitive; Adams writes, "He was small, with wide, staring eyes and a way of raising and turning his head which suggests not so much caution as a kind of ceaseless, nervous tension."

As the reader finds out, Fiver has a reason to be tense: he has had horrible visions of destruction. He sees the field where their warren is located covered with blood, and feels an overwhelming sense of death and danger all around them. He tells his brother Hazel about these visions, and urges that all the rabbits immediately evacuate the warren and go elsewhere. Because rabbit society is hierarchical, they must go see the Chief Rabbit and try to convince him; without his support, little can be done. The Chief Rabbit is reasonably fair, but has grown complacent in his leadership and is not inclined to listen to the ravings of a runt, especially since there is no concrete evidence of danger. The rabbits are content, there are no predators, the weather is good—in his mind, Fiver is to be pitied and patronized, not believed.

Media Adaptations

- *Watership Down* was adapted as an animated motion picture, produced by Martin Rosen of Nepenthe Productions and directed by John Hubley and Martin Rosen, in 1978. Voice actors included Joss Ackland as the Black Rabbit, Richard Briers as Fiver, Michael Graham-Cox as Bigwig, Micheal Hordern as Frith and the narrator, and John Hurt as Hazel.

However, of course Fiver is right, and Hazel, who knows him well, believes him. With a small group of other rabbits, they leave the old warren at Sandleford and set out across country looking for a new home. Fiver has seen it in a vision, and it is a high, clean hill, known as Watership Down, from which they can see predators long before the predators see them, find abundant food, and be far from the developments of humans. As the rabbits travel, Fiver urges them on, even when they're reluctant, led astray, or attacked by enemies. Fiver's prophetic gifts, and his storytelling ability, save them more than once; his visions lead them to safety, warn them of danger, suggest new ways of coping with trouble, and offer hope when, rationally, there is none.

Fiver's gift is passed on to one of his offspring,

a young rabbit who shows signs of his clairvoyance. Hazel, who has become leader of the new warren largely because of his faith in Fiver's gifts, says that as long as there are rabbits with this gift in the warren, the community as a whole will do well.

Hazel

Hazel is the leader of the rabbits who escape from Sandleford Warren after his brother Fiver warns that it will soon be destroyed; although other rabbits, including the Chief Rabbit of Sandleford, are skeptical about Fiver's warning, Hazel believes his brother and makes plans to leave. Hazel is a yearling and has not yet become a strong figure in the warren, although, as Adams writes, "He looked as though he knew how to take care of himself. There was a shrewd, buoyant air about him as he sat up, looked around and rubbed both paws over his nose." Hazel is calm, steady, and modest, as well as compassionate and fair, and as leader of the group, he encourages democratic discussion and listening to all the members of the group before making a decision. He does not always make good decisions —one that leads to trouble is his decision to get female rabbits from a nearby farm—but in general, he has balanced judgment. Eventually, he becomes the much-loved and respected leader, or Chief Rabbit, of the new warren on Watership Down.

At the end of the book, an epilogue shows Hazel lying half-asleep in his burrow when a shining stranger appears and summons him out into the spring sunshine. Although Adams does not state this explicitly, the text implies that this stranger is Lord Frith, the rabbit god, summoning him to the next world; evidently Hazel, having lived a long, eventful, and good life, has a peaceful death. As he passes some does and young rabbits on his way out, Adams writes, "he stopped for a moment to watch his rabbits and to try to get used to the extraordinary feeling that strength and speed were flowing inexhaustibly out of him into their sleek young bodies and healthy senses."

Holly

Holly is the captain of the Owsla, or security force, at the Sandleford Warren, under the leadership of the Chief Rabbit. He does not leave with the original group of rabbits, and in fact tries to arrest Bigwig and prevent him from leaving. When the bulldozers come and humans pipe poison gas into the warren, Holly escapes with one other survivor, a jester named Bluebell, and eventually finds the wanderers and joins Hazel's warren. He was originally deeply against their leaving Sandleford, but once he sees that they were right, he becomes an equally strong supporter of the new warren and Hazel's leadership in it, and even apologizes to Bigwig for trying to arrest him. He leads the initial expedition to Efrafa to get female rabbits, and barely escapes—without the does—but despite this experience is a strong fighter and leader throughout the book.

Hrairoo

See Fiver

Kehaar

Kehaar is a seagull who has been grounded by an injured wing near the Watership Down warren. When the rabbits find him, they are afraid of him at first, because most large birds prey on rabbits, but he is weak from starvation, and Hazel decides that they will help him and thus make an ally of him. Eventually, Hazel hopes, the bird can fly far and wide, find female rabbits, and tell the Watership Down rabbits where they are so that they can go get them and bring them back to join the warren. Kehaar is tough, blunt, intelligent, and social, and he is lonely now that the rest of his flock has migrated far away; although he has never socialized with rabbits before, he is happy to have others to talk to and perfectly willing to help them. He eventually finds does—at nearby Nuthanger Farm and at Efrafa. In their later confrontation with the rabbits of Efrafa, Kehaar acts as scout and spy, telling them of the enemy rabbits' movements and whereabouts as well as the layout of the terrain and carrying news back and forth from Bigwig, who is living undercover at Efrafa, and the other rabbits. He also attacks General Woundwort during his epic chase of Bigwig.

Strawberry

Strawberry is a large buck rabbit, a member of the highly civilized warren kept by a local farmer, and until his mate is killed by the farmer's snare, is a supporter of its system. When the Watership Down rabbits decide to leave, he comes with them, having realized that the price of food and safety—his mate's life—is too high to pay. He would rather live free, in the wild, and later proves to be a useful scout and fighter and a dependable member of the community.

Thlayli

See Bigwig

The Threarah

Also known as the Chief Rabbit, he is the leader of Sandleford Warren, and he has grown complacent in his power. When Hazel and Fiver come to him and tell him of Fiver's vision that the warren will be destroyed, he patronizes them and ignores their warning. "These rabbits," he says later, "who claim to have the second sight—I've known one or two in my time. But it's not usually advisable to take much notice of them." When he finds out that several rabbits have left, he sends the Sandleford security force after them, but when they come back empty-handed, he says there is no point in looking further. When Fiver's prophecy comes true and the warren is destroyed, two rabbits escape and eventually meet up with the Watership Down rabbits, but the Chief is not one of them; he does not survive the disaster.

General Woundwort

General Woundwort is the totalitarian dictator of the evil warren of Efrafa, a closed society which rabbits may enter but never leave. Like similar human societies, it has a repressive force of secret police and elaborate, brutal laws, and punishes infractions of them with torture and death. Woundwort was orphaned in infancy, grew up without love or community, and ended up savage, brutal, and with a lust for power and control. He is "almost as big as a hare and there's something about his mere presence that frightens you, as if blood and fighting and killing were all just part of the day's work to him." Woundwort forced himself into a small warren, quickly took control of it, and in time organized it into the feared warren of Efrafa. Supposedly, the elaborate repressive system of this warren is a method of keeping the rabbits from being detected and killed by humans and other enemies, and the members of the warren at first accepted this rationale. Woundwort established a ruling Council and strong-handed Owsla, both of which obeyed his commands without question. However, by the time the rabbits from Watership Down arrive, Efrafa has become overcrowded, and some rabbits are chafing against Woundwort's repressive regime.

After lengthy battles, Woundwort is finally defeated when the Watership Down rabbits lead a dog to attack him. His death is as brutal as his life was; at the end, as the dog bears down on him, he screams to his forces, "Come back, you fools! Dogs aren't dangerous! Come back and fight!" His body is never found, and eventually he becomes a sort of "bogey-man" to the local rabbits. Adams writes, "And mother rabbits would tell their kittens that if they did not do as they were told, the General would get them—the General who was first cousin to the Black Rabbit himself. Such was Woundwort's monument: and perhaps it would not have displeased him."

Themes

The Natural World and Development

A major concern in the book is the devastation of the natural world that results from human development of the land. The book's action begins when humans post a notice in the field where the rabbits live; it reads:

> THIS IDEALLY SITUATED ESTATE, COMPRISING SIX ACRES OF EXCELLENT BUILDING LAND, IS TO BE DEVELOPED WITH HIGH CLASS MODERN RESIDENCES BY SUTCH AND MARTIN, LIMITED, OF NEWBURY, BERKS.

In a harrowing chapter, one of the two survivors of the poisoning and bulldozing of the rabbits' home warren tells of the cold destruction, and the rabbits' realization that the humans killed them, as another rabbit said, "just because we were in their way. They killed us to suit themselves."

Throughout the book, the rabbits are keenly aware of humans and their disastrous effects. When they cross a road, Adams vividly describes the disgusting smells of cigarettes, tar, gasoline, and exhaust, as well as the rabbits' nauseated response to them. The cars on the road can run faster than any rabbit—something highly unnatural—and when they pass a rabbit, they don't seem to notice the rabbit at all. Machinelike, they stay on the road, and machinelike, they don't slow down for animals. This lesson of human senselessness and lack of connection or care is borne out by the presence of a smashed piece of roadkill—a hedgehog that is now "a flattened, bloody mass of brown prickles and white fur, with small black feet and snout crushed round the edges."

Humans are associated with this senseless, machinelike response to the world, which leads to callous death; they are also associated with some of the worst enemies of rabbits: cats and dogs. In contrast, Adams lovingly and vividly describes the natural world in great detail. Almost every page of the book contains passages on nature that are as vivid as those written by any naturalist and that allow the reader to step into the rabbits' world. In fact the book begins, "The primroses were over. Toward the edge of the wood, where the ground became open and sloped down to an old fence and a brambly ditch beyond, only a few fading patches of pale yellow still showed among the dog's mercury and oak-tree roots. On the other side of the fence, the ground was full of rabbit holes...."

Throughout the book, descriptions of natural beauty and rabbit life are contrasted with the disastrous effects of humanity. The first warren is utterly destroyed by development. Cowslip's warren, where the rabbits are fat and leisurely, is owned by a farmer, who kills rabbits to sell for meat. Efrafa, the totalitarian dictatorship, became that way partly in response to hazards—if humans didn't know the rabbits were there, they couldn't kill them, so General Woundwort instituted an increasingly repressive series of controls to keep the warren a secret. Kehaar the seagull is wounded by a farmer's pet cat, and so is Hazel.

The rabbits' only chance for permanent safety lies in getting as far away from humans as possible —to the remote, high country of Watership Down. What Adams does not bring up is the question of whether increasing development will eventually reach even there—if the rabbits' safe home will one day, like the first warren, be destroyed to make way for human building.

Topics for Further Study

- How is General Woundwort like other dictators in human history?

What methods does he use to control his community, and how are these similar to methods that have been used in repressive regimes throughout history? Do you think that his experience of an unhappy youth fully explains his actions?

- When the Watership Down rabbits meet Cowslip, they find that his community has highly developed art, poetry, and architecture, and that these rabbits look down on the religious beliefs and mythological tales the less-sophisticated Watership Down rabbits share. Are there parallels between these rabbit societies and others in human history? For instance, when Europeans first met native people throughout the world, how did they view the spiritual beliefs and customs of these people in comparison to their own?

- The rabbits in Cowslip's warren pay a price for their high standard of living: they have lost their freedom. If someone offered you all the wealth and comfort you ever dreamed of in exchange for your freedom (and perhaps someday, your life or that of someone you love), would you take it? Why or why not?

- *Watership Down* speaks strongly against development, and strongly for the preservation of the environment and the habitat of animals. In the book, the animals are the heroes and humans are shortsighted and greedy. Is there a place near you that has been destroyed by development, as the rabbits' home warren was? What was it like before, and what is it like now? Are shopping malls, suburban developments, parking lots, golf courses, and other places worth the price of losing wild land?

- Adams creates a whole world for his rabbit characters, with its own language, customs, mythology, and spiritual beliefs. These are based loosely on real, observed characteristics of rabbits as described by naturalist R. M. Lockley, whom Adams often quotes in the book. Choose an animal of your own and invent a language and society for it, basing these on real characteristics of the animal as described by naturalists.

Democracy versus Totalitarianism

The book clearly contrasts two forms of leadership—democratic versus totalitarian. Under Hazel's leadership, discussion, openness, and equal participation among all members of the warren is encouraged. In the closed warren of Efrafa, General Woundwort's word is law, and any discussion is immediately punished.

In Efrafa, each rabbit is "marked," and its behavior is strictly regulated; as Holly explains, "They bite them, deep, and under the chin or in a haunch or forepaw. Then they can be told by the scar for the rest of their lives. You mustn't be found above ground [to feed or excrete waste] unless it's the right time of day for your Mark." Each Mark has a captain who oversees this and punishes infractions, and if a Mark can't go aboveground because a man or a predator is near, it must wait until the next day. To prevent the spread of infection—and dissension—rabbits are not allowed to visit another Mark's burrows without permission, which is seldom granted.

The warren's Owsla, or police, patrol the countryside, watching out for predators. When they find strange rabbits, they bring them back to Efrafa or, if they won't come back, kill them so that they don't attract the attention of humans or other predators to the area.

Supposedly, this system arose because General Woundwort, who took control of the warren, wanted to ensure its safety from predators.

However, in exchange for safety from outside enemies, the rabbits now are constantly threatened and oppressed from within, by those in power. As a result, most of the rabbits in the warren can't do anything but what they're told to do; they've never been out of the warren, never smelled an enemy, and never learned to think independently.

Those who do think independently are severely punished. In a chilling incident, Bigwig meets Blackavar, a rabbit who tried to leave Efrafa. Guarded by rabbit officers, he stands at the entrance to a burrow, where all can see him. As Adams writes, "He was dreadfully mutilated. His ears were nothing but shapeless shreds, ragged at the edges, seamed with ill-knit scars and beaded here and there with lumps of proud, bare flesh. One eyelid was misshapen and closed askew." He has been held here for a month, forced to explain to all who ask that this torture and mutilation was his punishment for attempting to leave, and thus instilling fear and obedience in other possible rebels.

Style

Myths and Tales

A most unusual feature of the book is its depiction of rabbits' mythological and spiritual life. Throughout *Watership Down*, chapters telling tales of rabbit adventures are interspersed with stories of another kind—legends from the rabbit mythology. The rabbits tell each other tales of how the first rabbit, El-ahrairah, received a white tail and strong back legs from Frith, the sun god, and at the same time, was marked as prey for many other animals. "All the world will be your enemy, Prince with a Thousand Enemies, and whenever they catch you, they will kill you. But first they must catch you, digger, listener, runner, prince with the swift warning." Other stories tell how El-ahrairah stole the king's lettuce; how he was put on trial for stealing Prince Rainbow's carrots; how, when his people were under siege, he went to the Black Rabbit of Inle (Death personified) and offered his own life in exchange for the safety of his people; how he outwitted a huge dog, and other tales. All these stories serve to reinforce the rabbits' sense of a shared heritage. They also reinforce the rabbits' view of themselves as fast, cunning, compassionate, and community-minded. Traditional rabbit virtues are like old-fashioned human ones: the hero El-ahrairah is ready to help his companions, give up his own life for them, and fight for what he believes in. At the same time, he is quick, cunning, has a bright sense of humor, and is a consummate storyteller, all traits the rabbits value highly. These myths help bond the rabbits together in times of trouble, and also inspire them with ideas to use in their own difficulties.

Naturalistic Detail

Another feature, as notable as Adams's use of myth and exactly opposite from it, is his use of closely observed, factual details of rabbit life and nature. Many of the epigrams preceding chapters are drawn from the naturalist R. M. Lockley's book *The Private Life of the Rabbit*, which Adams also cites in his acknowledgments. Adams clearly used this book to inspire and inform his descriptions of rabbit behavior and "customs." He was also a keen observer of many other aspects of natural phenomena, including weather, flowering times, the movements and appearance of insects, and the habitats of various birds and plants. A list of all the birds, plants, animals, and insects he mentions would probably comprise a relatively complete field guide to the part of England where the story is set.

As the rabbits travel across country, Adams also keenly observes and describes the smells, textures, and fauna of the different territories they cover, from the damp river bank to the mysterious and dangerous forest, to the peaty, boggy, rocky upland, to the high, clean height of Watership Down. All these places are real—though of course the characters are not—and these rich details serve to ground the reader in Adams's setting, give the story authority, and encourage the reader to believe in the "truth" of the tale.

Animal Communication

Another interesting feature of the book is that in Adams's world, rabbits can communicate with each other and with other animals, although communication with other animals takes place through a sort of universal pidgin, or primitive language, which all the animals use when talking to other species. The one "animal" who cannot understand the rabbits, and whom the rabbits can't understand, is the human. In Adams's world, humans are outside the natural order and even in opposition to it—their presence almost invariably leads to death and destruction. (The one exception to this is Lucy, the farmer's daughter, who saves Hazel and insists that the doctor bring him back to the warren in his car; perhaps this is because she is a child, and therefore still innocent and perhaps closer to the animals than adult humans are.) The book reverses the usual perception of animals as "dumb" creatures that cannot feel or communicate; in it, humans are the senseless, speechless ones. They kill without thinking, and unlike natural predators such as foxes who kill to survive, they simply roll on in their cars, or build their developments, without even noticing the devastation they've caused.

A Created World

Watership Down is set in the larger human world of Berkshire in England, but the historical time in which it takes place is vague. The events clearly take place sometime in the second half of the twentieth century, since cars and trucks are commonplace, and age-old fields and farms are threatened by development. However, Adams is not interested in the human world or in human history. The rabbits are the focus of the story, and of course don't know of historical events in the human world, so this aspect of the story is deliberately left vague. This gives the book an immediacy and refreshing lack of datedness that it would not have if Adams had identified the time period: the book could be taking place now, or in the 1970s, when Adams wrote it.

The rabbits do have a history and a culture of their own, although their immediate history is not as detailed, since they don't write anything down. Rabbits may have heard stories of their grandfathers or grandmothers, but their history seldom goes back farther than that; events taking place any time earlier than that gradually become part of the mythic age of El-ahrairah, the rabbits' clever, trickster hero.

The book is set in an actual area in England;

Adams writes in a note at the beginning that "Nuthanger Farm is a real place, like all the other places in the book," but that the few humans mentioned in it are fictitious. In addition, Adams's close observation of place makes it evident that the places mentioned are real. Since the book was written almost three decades ago, it would be interesting for a reader, or for Adams, to go back now and note whether the landscape has changed—whether Watership Down is still safe from development, or whether the real farms, fields, and forests the fictional rabbits traveled through have changed through human intervention.

The culture of the Watership Down rabbits is similar to some traditional human cultures, with an emphasis on oral tradition and on tribal/community values such as heroism, self-sacrifice, community, family, and compassion, as well as democracy. Like human societies, however, rabbit culture and government differ from warren to warren, and as the rabbits discover, Efrafa is a physically and spiritually oppressive dictatorship. At the time Adams wrote the book, many nations lived under this type of system, most notably the Soviet Union and Eastern European countries, on which Efrafa seems to be modeled. The Cold War was still a very important factor in European and American consciousness, and people outside those countries were well aware that torture, killing, and imprisonment of dissidents was commonplace. Like Efrafa, these countries justified this oppression of their citizens with the rationale that their tight control was for the ultimate security and safety of all. Since Adams wrote *Watership Down*, the governments of many of these countries have become more democratic, but dictatorships still exist in many places in the world and the example of Efrafa is still relevant. Just as in Efrafa, history has shown that in these countries there will always be dissidents, attempts to escape, and discontent.

Critical Overview

People have probably been telling stories about animals since time began. Some of the earliest known animal stories are the fables of Aesop, a slave who lived in Greece around 500 B.C. He told stories about animals, which had morals illustrating lessons and aspects of human life. Since then, many authors have told and written stories in which animals could speak and talk, and in which they have their own societies. Some early, and still well known, animal stories include Rudyard Kipling's *Just So Stories* and *Jungle Book*, Joel Chandler Harris's *Uncle Remus* stories, Kenneth Grahame's *The Wind in the Willows*, and George Orwell's *Animal Farm*. However, these stories were not realistic in the sense that they did not take into account the actual biology and behavior of the animals: the characters were basically humans in animal form.

The first realistically told animal story was *Bambi*, by Felix Salten, a Hungarian journalist. Unlike the more famous Disney film, the book is not sentimental, but is, as Cathi Dunn MacRae wrote in *Presenting Young Adult Fantasy Fiction*, "a sensitive study of a deer's natural life. Joy and fear are basic expressions for Bambi and his forest companions; death is part of life. Salten's respect for animals' experience was revolutionary."

Like Salten, Adams bases his rabbit society on

many real characteristics of the biology and behavior of rabbits, particularly as they are described by naturalist R. M. Lockley in his classic *The Private Life of the Rabbit*, whom Adams often quotes in the epigraphs of chapters in the book.

In *A Reader's Guide to Fantasy*, Baird Searles, Beth Meacham, and Michael Franklin wrote that *Watership Down* "caused a sensation" when it came out, mainly because, unlike previous works such as *Bambi*, the book tells the rabbits' story in an epic context, and includes excerpts from the rabbit mythology. They also write, "There is also a healthy dose of satiric allegory, which fortunately does not dominate the novel."

Adams's success led to many others following in his footsteps and writing what have since become known as "animal fantasies." According to MacRae, this type of writing has several characteristics, including: (1) language and the ability to communicate with other species; (2) a culture that is not based on human values; (3) a visionary leader who senses dangers and leads the group toward change; (4) an underlying sense that animals are superior to brutal humans; and (5) a struggle for survival against a force, often of human origin, that threatens their way of life. As MacRae noted, *Watership Down* has been so successful, and incorporated these traits so completely, that "few animal fantasies escape comparison."

Critics have differed, however, on how effective the use of these typical conventions really is. In *Fantasy Literature: A Core Collection and*

Reference Guide, Marshall B. Tymn, Kenneth J. Zahorski, and Robert H. Boyer wrote that the main reason for the success of the book is that people are charmed by stories of animals that can talk. "This charm," they wrote, "as well as the spell of a well-told tale, is what has made [the book] so popular."

Peter Hunt wrote in the *International Companion Encyclopedia of Children's Literature*, "Its intricate depiction of a rabbit community and the characterization of its (mainly male) protagonists have enough contact with realism to make the book seem entirely credible."

However, in *Fantasy and Mimesis: Responses to Reality in Western Literature*, Kathryn Hume wrote that in her opinion, the book starts out attempting to enter rabbit minds, "but quickly lets the lapine [rabbit] vocabulary ... substitute for real strangeness, while the plot degenerates into the adventures of animals with human brains.... The novelty and strangeness which entering a rabbit's mind should entail quickly disappears. The fantasy of this adventure is only skin deep; the minds and characters of these furry humans are but little touched by newness or originality."

In *National Review*, D. Keith Mano wrote in response to another critic's comment that the book did not fit any known formula, "Nonsense: it fits five or six. This bunny squad could be a John Wayne platoon of GIs. The foresighted, tactful rabbit leader. The fast rabbit. The clever rabbit. The blustery, hard-fighting noncom rabbit.... *Watership Down* is pleasant enough, but it has about the same intellectual firepower as *Dumbo*.... This is an okay book; well enough written. But it is grossly overrated."

Despite the criticisms of Mano and others, readers loved the book, sending it to the best-seller lists and leading it to be regarded as a classic of modern fantasy. In the *New York Review of Books*, Alison Lurie wrote that the reason the book was so successful and so loved was that unlike many contemporary novels, which feature sad, cynical, or nasty characters, *Watership Down* celebrates characters "who have honor and courage and dignity, who will risk their lives for others, [and] whose love for their families and friends and community is enduring and effective."

The book's popularity has endured, and since its publication, there has been a surge in the publication of animal fantasies; readers can now read books starring sentient horses, foxes, cats, and many other animals, thanks to Adams's groundbreaking work.

Sources

Campbell, Joseph, *Hero with a Thousand Faces*, Bollingen, 1949.

Clift, Jean Dalby, and Wallace B. Clift, *The Archetype of Pilgrimage*, Paulist Press, 1996.

Hume, Kathryn, *Fantasy and Mimesis: Responses to Reality in Western Literature*, Methuen, 1984.

Hunt, Peter, ed., *International Companion Encyclopedia of Children's Literature*, Routledge, 1996.

Levoy, Gregg, *Callings*, Three Rivers Press, 1997.

Lurie, Alison, Review, in *New York Review of Books*, April 18, 1974.

MacRae, Cathi Dunn, *Presenting Young Adult Fantasy Fiction*, Twayne Publishers, 1998.

Mano, D. Keith, Review, in *National Review*, April 26, 1974.

Rawicz, Slavomir, *The Long Walk: The True Story of a Trek to Freedom*, Lyons Press, 1956.

Searles, Baird, Beth Meacham, and Michael Franklin, *A Reader's Guide to Fantasy*, Facts on File, 1982.

Tymn, Marshall B., Kenneth J. Zahorski, and Robert H. Boyer, *Fantasy Literature: A Core Collection and Reference Guide*, R. R. Bowker, 1979.

For Further Study

Adams, Richard, *The Day Gone By*, Century Hutchinson, 1990.

Adams's autobiography.

Helbig, Alethea K., and Agnes Regan Perkins, *Dictionary of British Children's Fiction: Books of Recognized Merit*, Vol. 1: A-M, Greenwood Press, 1989.

Provides a biography of Adams.

Smith, Elliot Fremont, Review, in *New York*, March 4, 1974.

Review of *Watership Down*.